Weather

Fog

by Helen Frost

Consulting Editor: Gail Saunders-Smith, Ph.D.
Consultant: Joseph M. Moran, Ph.D., Meteorologist
Associate Director, Education Program
American Meteorological Society
Washington, D.C.

Capstone
press

Mankato, Minnesota

Pebble Books are published by Capstone Press
151 Good Counsel Drive, P.O. Box 669, Mankato, Minnesota 56002
www.capstonepress.com

1 2 3 4 5 6 09 08 07 06 05 04

Library of Congress Cataloging-in-Publication Data
Frost, Helen, 1949–
    Fog / by Helen Frost.
    p. cm.—(Weather)
    Summary: Simple text and photographs present fog, how it is formed, and how
it affects the Earth and people.
    Includes bibliographical references and index.
    ISBN 0-7368-2093-0 (hardcover)
    1. Fog—Juvenile literature. [1. Fog.] I. Title. II. Series: Weather (Mankato, Minn.)
QC929.F7F76 2004
551.57′5—dc22   2003013404

Note to Parents and Teachers

The Weather series supports national science standards related
to earth science. This book describes and illustrates fog. The
photographs support early readers in understanding the text. The
repetition of words and phrases helps early readers learn new
words. This book also introduces early readers to subject-specific
vocabulary words, which are defined in the Glossary. Early readers
may need assistance to read some words and to use the Table of
Contents, Glossary, Read More, Internet Sites, and Index/Word List
sections of the book.

Table of Contents

What Is Fog?

Fog is a cloud close to land or water. People cannot see well in fog.

Fog forms in humid air.
Humid air holds water
vapor. Water vapor is
a gas that cannot be seen.

Water vapor turns into droplets of water when air cools. These droplets can be seen as fog.

Kinds of Fog

Radiation fog forms when warm humid air cools. This kind of fog forms close to the ground.

Advection fog forms when warm humid air moves over cold water or land. This kind of fog looks like it is rolling in.

14

Ice fog forms in very cold places. Water vapor turns into tiny ice crystals. The ice crystals stay in the air as fog.

What Fog Does

Thick fog hides everything. Trucks, school buses, and cars move slowly in thick fog. Airplanes cannot take off or land in fog.

People on ships cannot see through thick fog. Lighthouses shine lights through fog and darkness. Loud foghorns blow to warn ships when they are near land.

Fog disappears when the air warms or the wind blows. The water droplets change back into water vapor. People can see again.

Glossary

advection fog—a kind of fog that forms when warm humid air moves over cold water or land

crystal—a solid substance having a regular pattern of many flat surfaces

foghorn—a loud horn used to warn ships in foggy weather and in darkness

gas—a substance that will spread to fill any space that contains it

humid—wet; humid air holds a lot of water vapor.

lighthouse—a tower near the sea; a lighthouse has a flashing light at the top to guide ships or to warn ships of danger.

radiation fog—a kind of fog that forms when warm humid air cools

vapor—a gas formed from something that is a liquid or a solid at other temperatures

Read More

Eckart, Edana. *Watching the Weather.* Watching Nature. New York: Children's Press, 2004.

Frost, Helen. *Water as a Gas.* Water. Mankato, Minn.: Pebble Books, 2000.

Weber, Rebecca. *Weather Wise.* Spyglass Books. Minneapolis: Compass Point Books, 2003.

Internet Sites

FactHound offers a safe, fun way to find Internet sites related to this book. All of the sites on FactHound have been researched by our staff.

Here's how:

1. Visit *www.facthound.com*

2. Type in this special code **0736820930** for age-appropriate sites. Or enter a search word related to this book for a more general search.

3. Click on the **Fetch It** button.

FactHound will fetch the best sites for you!

Index/Word List

Word Count: 184
Early-Intervention Level: 18

Editorial Credits

Martha E. H. Rustad, editor; Timothy Halldin, series designer; Molly Nei, book designer; Deirdre Barton, photo researcher; Karen Risch, product planning editor

Photo Credits

Brand X Pictures/Bob Rashid/Tony Baker, 4; Brand X Pictures/David Lorenz Winston, 8; Corbis/Galen Rowell, 12; Corbis/Gunter Marx Photography, 20; Digital Vision/Nat Photos & Tony Sweet, cover, 14; Steven J. Meunier, 1; Unicorn Stock Photos/Aneal Vohra, 16; Unicorn Stock Photos/David Fox, 6; Unicorn Stock Photos/Gary L. Johnson, 10; Unicorn Stock Photos/Thomas H. Mitchell, 18

The author thanks the children's library staff at the Allen County Public Library in Fort Wayne, Indiana, for research assistance.